Love & Friendship

Adventures in Ink & Inspiration

This is a FLAME TREE book | First published 2016

Publisher and Creative Director: Nick Wells
Senior Project Editor: Laura Bulbeck
Digital Manager: Chris Herbert
Art Director: Mike Spender

Special thanks to Frances Bodiam

Images in this book were crafted at the Flame Tree Studio, based on illustrations
© copyright 578foot, Tania Anisimova, art_of_sun, Attsetski, De-V, Jake Jackson, Elena
Melnikova, joinanita, Lindwa, Mikhaylova Liubov, Marina99, MarushaBelle,
nata_danilenko, Tashsat, tets.

© Flame Tree Publishing Ltd 2016

FLAME TREE PUBLISHING
6 Melbray Mews, Fulham,
London SW6 3NS, United Kingdom

www.flametreepublishing.com

ISBN 978-1-78361-911-5

1 3 5 7 9 10 8 6 4 2
16 18 20 19 17

Printed in China | Created and designed in the UK

Love & Friendship

Adventures in Ink & Inspiration

Words & Selection by Daisy Seal
Created by the Flame Tree Studio

FLAME TREE
PUBLISHING

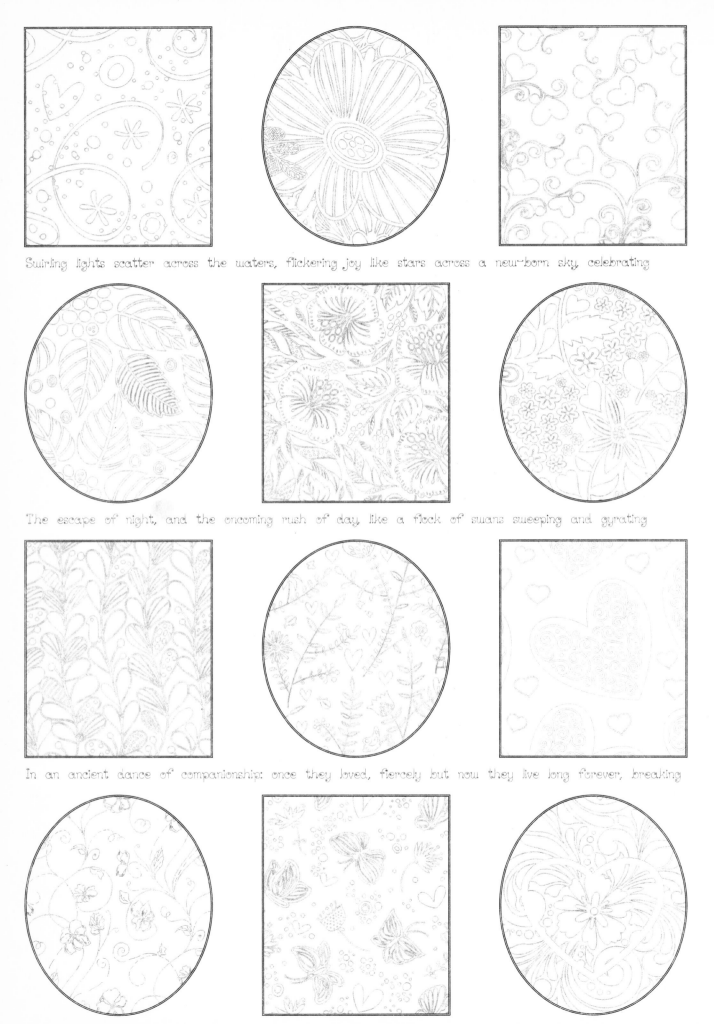

Swirling lights scatter across the waters, flickering joy like stars across a new-born sky, celebrating

The escape of night, and the oncoming rush of day, like a flock of swans sweeping and gyrating

In an ancient dance of companionship: once they loved, fiercely but now they live long forever, breaking

The spray of the waters of life, the past rolling with the future, ever-present in the dreaming and waking.

Love & Friendship

Adventures in Ink & Inspiration

Easy, intermediate and challenging this wonderful new book will give you hours of calm entertainment. Packed with delightful images, this time we've added a series of inspirational messages for love and friendship which emerge from the swirling backgrounds.

Love & Friendship will take you on a journey through the whirl of life and companionship. We all dream of falling in love, and we all need good friends to help us through the difficult times, and celebrate the best of life too. The thoughtful sayings can offer moments of reflection for our busy day, as we wake with the warm sun on our faces, battle through the chores of family and work, then drift with nightfall into sleep, dreaming, perhaps, of friendship and love.

As with the previous books Secret Places, Woodland Places and the companion to this title, Mindfulness & Calm, you can use a variety of pens: from gel and pencil, to pigment and crayon, from ballpoint and rollerball to highlighters, although it's best to avoid the heavy felt pens.

We designed the book so you can either colour the page with the hidden messages, or the image on the back, which is the same but without the words. Each page is perforated near the spine, so you can tear them out carefully and frame, perhaps even send them as a gift to a loved one.

Don't forget to sign your name at the bottom of the page, when you've finished each picture...

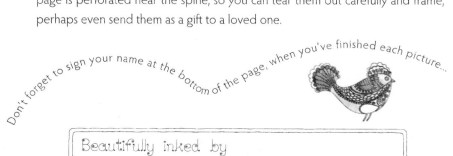

Beautifully inked by

Beautifully inked by

SUCH SOFT,
SWEET SMILES
ARE MADE FROM
YOUR GENTLE
STRENGTHS

Beautifully inked by

Beautifully inked by

YOUR FRIENDS WILL ALWAYS STAND TALL FOR YOU

Beautifully inked by

Beautifully inked by

OUR LOVE HAS GROWN WITH THE TENDERNESS OF A SUMMER'S BREEZE

Beautifully inked by

Beautifully inked by

A RAINBOW CANNOT MATCH YOUR BEAUTY OR THE MODESTY OF YOUR GESTURES.

Beautifully inked by

Beautifully inked by

IN ONE MOMENT WE CAN STEAL AN ETERNITY OF TIME TOGETHER.

Beautifully inked by

Beautifully inked by

Beautifully inked by

FROM THE TIPS OF MY TOES TO THE TINGLE AT THE END OF MY FINGERS.

Beautifully inked by

Beautifully inked by

WILL YOU BE MINE, TO LOVE UNTIL THE MOON IS TOO EXHAUSTED TO RISE AGAIN?

Beautifully inked by

Beautifully inked by

A KIND WORD CAN RETURN WITH A FRIEND MANY YEARS LATER

Beautifully inked by

Beautifully inked by

AN ANGEL QUIETLY AT REST YOU LOOK SO BEAUTIFUL WHEN YOU SLEEP

Beautifully inked by

Beautifully inked by

EVEN A QUIET LOVE CAN BE POWERFUL AND LONG-LASTING.

Beautifully inked by

Beautifully inked by

EVEN A SINGLE WORD FROM YOU CAN MAKE ME FEEL LIKE DANCING FOR A WEEK.

Beautifully inked by

Beautifully inked by

YOU HAVE A BEAUTY SO PURE AND TRUE THAT I'M HUMBLED BY YOUR LOVE.

Beautifully inked by

Beautifully inked by

THERE ARE TIMES IN THE DAY, WHEN I THINK ONLY OF YOU

Beautifully inked by

Beautifully inked by

SOMETIMES I THINK UPON YOUR SMILE, AND THE WAY YOU BRUSH THE HAIR FROM YOUR EYES.

Beautifully inked by

Beautifully inked by

Beautifully inked by

WE CELEBRATE OUR FRIENDSHIP, WITH SMILES AND GENTLE LAUGHTER.

Beautifully inked by

Beautifully inked by

RELAX INTO MY ARMS AS WE SINK INTO THE YEARS

Beautifully inked by

Beautifully inked by

THOUGHTS OF YOU BRING MEMORIES OF PETALS DRIFTING IN A BREEZE.

Beautifully inked by

Beautifully inked by

YOUR BEAUTY, AS DELICATE AS YOUR BREATH UPON THE WINDOW.

Beautifully inked by

Beautifully inked by

AS WE GROW
TOGETHER,
OUR LOVE
GROWS TOO.

Beautifully inked by

Beautifully inked by

THE INTENSITY OF YOUTH PULSES STILL WITHIN THE CONTENTMENT OF OLD AGE.

Beautifully inked by

Beautifully inked by

FRIENDSHIPS LAST UNTIL THE SUN IS TOO OLD TO BRUSH AWAY THE STARS.

Beautifully inked by

Beautifully inked by

THOUGHTS OF YOU BRING MEMORIES OF PETALS DRIFTING IN A BREEZE.

Beautifully inked by

Beautifully inked by

LOVE CAN TAKE MANY FORMS, FROM RAGING GLORY TO A QUIET ROAR.

Beautifully inked by

Beautifully inked by

I WAIT TO SEE YOU AGAIN, MY BREATH IS TOO SHY TO WAIT TOO.

Beautifully inked by

Beautifully inked by

WHEN I AM WITHOUT YOU I TRACE YOUR FACE IN THE AIR AND WATCH YOU SMILE BACK AT ME

Beautifully inked by

Beautifully inked by

WHEN YOU HOLD MY HAND, I FEEL WARMED BY A THOUSAND FRIENDS.

Beautifully inked by

Beautifully inked by

SOMETIMES, WHEN I THINK OF YOU, MY HEART BLOOMS WITH PRIDE.

Beautifully inked by

Beautifully inked by

FRIENDS ARE LIKE PETALS ON A MEADOW FLOWER, AT ONCE DELICATE YET STRONG.

Beautifully inked by

Beautifully inked by

YOUR FRIENDSHIP IS TALL AND STRONG. WE ARE MANY TOGETHER FACING THE WORLD.

Beautifully inked by

Beautifully inked by

Beautifully inked by

FRIENDSHIPS HELP YOU SHARE THE GOOD TIMES, AS WELL AS THE BAD.

Beautifully inked by

Beautifully inked by

A KIND WORD
CAN RETURN WITH
A FRIEND MANY
YEARS LATER

Beautifully inked by

Beautifully inked by

ALTHOUGH LIFE FLEES SWIFTLY OUR LOVE IS LIKE A ROCK, AROUND WHICH TIME FLOWS.

Beautifully inked by

Beautifully inked by

WE ALL APPRECIATE THE SIMPLE BEAUTY OF FRIENDSHIP

Beautifully inked by

Beautifully inked by

SOME PEOPLE ONLY FIND ONE TRUE FRIEND : THAT SHOULD BE MORE THAN ENOUGH!

Beautifully inked by

Beautifully inked by

MY FOOLISH HEART HAS CAPTURED MY BREATH UNTIL YOU RETURN.

Beautifully inked by

Beautifully inked by

OUR LOVE IS LIKE THE OCEAN, WITH ITS TIDAL WAVES RISING & FALLING WITH THE SEASONS.

Beautifully inked by

Beautifully inked by

A FRIENDSHIP OF THE LIKE-MINDED IS A TREASURE THAT WILL LAST A LIFETIME

Beautifully inked by

Beautifully inked by

STRONG FRIENDSHIPS CAN BE FOUND IN COMMON APPRECIATION.

Beautifully inked by

Beautifully inked by

FRIENDSHIP IS A COMPLEX MIX OF INTIMACY AND FREEDOM.

Beautifully inked by

Beautifully inked by

IT'S MUCH EASIER TO LET FRIENDSHIPS GROW NATURALLY, THAN TO SEEK THEM TOO FIERCELY.

Beautifully inked by

Beautifully inked by

Beautifully inked by

Beautifully inked by

Beautifully inked by

Beautifully inked by

IT IS OFTEN THE QUIET, MODEST FRIENDSHIPS THAT ARE THE MOST ENDURING.

Beautifully inked by

Beautifully inked by

YOUR QUIET SUPPORT HAS BROUGHT DAYLIGHT INTO THE SHADOWS OF MY MIND

Beautifully inked by

Beautifully inked by

YESTERDAY I THOUGHT OF YOU, A SUNRISE WARMING THE SLEEP FROM MY EYES

Beautifully inked by

Beautifully inked by

YOUR KINDNESS AND GENEROSITY WILL LIVE WITH ME FOREVER.

Beautifully inked by

Beautifully inked by

SOMETIMES, JUST A SIMPLE THANK YOU WILL DO.

Beautifully inked by

Beautifully inked by

GREETING YOU TODAY IS A DIFFERENT PERSON THANKS MOSTLY TO YOU

Beautifully inked by

Beautifully inked by

YOUR FRIENDSHIP HAS FOUND THE LIGHT I THOUGHT HAD DRAINED FROM MY LIFE

Beautifully inked by

Beautifully inked by

TIME IS SUCH A
BEAUTIFUL GIFT
YOU HAVE BEEN
SO GENEROUS
WITH YOURS

Beautifully inked by

Beautifully inked by

THANK YOU FOR HELPING ME SEE THE WORLD AS IT TRULY IS, NOT AS I FEARED IT MIGHT BE.

Beautifully inked by

Beautifully inked by

YOUR DELICATE INTERVENTIONS HAVE BROUGHT ME GENTLY BACK TO SANITY

Beautifully inked by

Beautifully inked by

Beautifully inked by

Beautifully inked by

Beautifully inked by

OUR FRIENDSHIP IS LIKE THE MOST SUBLIME OF SUNSETS

Beautifully inked by

Beautifully inked by

YOUR CLEAR COMMON SENSE HAS BRUSHED AWAY UNCERTAINTY.

Beautifully inked by

Visual Arts

FLAME TREE PUBLISHING
flametreepublishing.com

From **How to Draw Manga** to **Street Art**,
Alphonse Mucha to **Drawing Basics**, we publish
a range of fine and practical books, calendars and
foiled journals for artists and everyday enthusiasts.

If you enjoyed this book, please sign up for updates,
information and offers on further titles on the visual arts at
blog.flametreepublishing.com/art-of-fine-gifts/